Define Signature Style

Be Recognised for Who You Are

Berith Sandgren-Clarke

First Published in Great Britain 2019

By Berith Sandgren-Clarke

Copyright ©2019 by Berith Sandgren-Clarke

All rights reserved. This book or any portion thereof may not be reproduced or used in any manner whatsoever without the express written permission of the publisher except for the use of brief quotations in a book review.

Paperback ISBN: 978-1-095355-4-11

Berith Sandgren-Clarke
2B-inspired

www.2B-inspired.com

For Evelyn and Rosanna

Define Your Signature Style

Your signature style is an extension of your innermost being – a personalised style that's free from pretence or deceit. A style that will be created and claimed when your confidence in who you are reflects your values as well as your vision and mission in life. The way you present yourself is important; it's the only marketing tool that you have 100% control over. However, most entrepreneurial women are unaware of how to use this knowledge to best effect without defeating the aim of being authentic.

Where to start:

- Before you get to a place of confidence you need to know what's holding you back, creating tools that will move you forward.

- You need to understand what makes you the person you are: what you are passionate about, what you want to achieve and what you are willing to do to get to that new place

- When your vision, values and mission are aligned you can start to claim your signature style.

- Having a signature style has nothing to do with following fashion; it has everything to do with understanding what you would never compromise on - to know how to wear what suits you.

Being remembered as someone with a strong personalised style is powerful and will give others a secure feeling that you have integrity whist being honest and true to who you are.

It's time to Define Who You Are.

Claim Your FREE 20-minute Style Audit by taking the Confidence Calculator Assessment HERE and NOW >>

https://www.2b-inspired.com/the-assessment

Contents

Foreword	9
Introduction	13
A Wise Decision	19
Know Thyself	27
True Representation	35
Permission to Change	43
Never too Late	53
The Honest Truth	59
With Open Arms	67
A Burning Desire	75
A Work in Progress	85
To Be Inspired	93
You're My Best Friend	101
In the Right Direction	109
Here I am	117
Awareness Unleashed	125
A True Bargain	133
Not 'The End'	141
What Next?	149
Footnote	151
Gratitude	155
Resources	157
Praise	159
About the Author	163
Further Inspiration	167

FOREWORD by Kezia

For as long as I can remember I have had a love hate relationship with clothes. The daily battle of opening the wardrobe, looking for inspiration, only to revert back to the safe, comfortable options half an hour later.

When I got older, I wrongly assumed that I would naturally discover what fitted my non-conforming body, with my broad shoulders, snake hips and short legs and with more money to spend on clothes than ever before I thought it would be easy to feel a million dollars.

However, the reality was in fact the total reverse, more expensive mistakes and more outfits that never saw the light of day, as I eventually resigned myself to a look that neither felt comfortable or inspiring and certainly did not reflect the powerful woman inside me screaming to get out.

The quote "Clothes maketh the man" also applies to women and knowing what to wear to enhance your body, your style and your features will not only boost your confidence and make you feel absolutely amazing but will save you thousands of pounds and create more space and time for those things that matter. Just imagine opening your wardrobe each morning knowing that everything inside flatters your body and reflects the woman you are on the inside.

Define your signature style – Be recognised for who you are, is an easy to read story of one woman's mission to discover and embrace her authentic style. With helpful tips and resources, it guides you to start consciously thinking about your own style and whether or not it truly represents the woman you are and want to be in the future and how you can take the necessary steps to create the change that you wish to see.

Berith Sandgren-Clarke's elegant beauty, timeless fashion and warm and inviting manner, supports women on this journey of discovering their signature style, enhancing and embracing it, giving women the confidence, they need to make a positive lasting impression in all areas of their life.

As when our outside world reflects our inside world, we hold our head up high, step out with confidence and truly make the contribution to the world we were destined to make. So, now before you start reading make a cup of tea, get comfortable and take the first step to reclaiming your signature style.

Kezia Luckett
Positive Psychologist, CEO & Trailblazer behind the Women of Contribution movement

FOREWORD by Robin

As a child, I have memories of friends, and even family, poking fun at me because of the unique colour combinations I used to wear.

It wasn't until I turned eight and went to the opticians for the first time that the kind-hearted optician informed my parents that I was colour blind. My mum looked over my bright green T-shirt and red corduroy trousers and, looking back now, I can remember seeing an, "Aha!" moment on her face.

We spent some time going through my wardrobe, and as I reached my teenage years my clothes became more neutral in colour: lots of greys, blue jeans, navy and black. That served me well right the way through my school and university years and finally into setting up my first business.

Yet...something still wasn't quite right. You would think that by now, as a 22-year-old, fully independent young man I would have created my own style and found my way around this annoying colour-blind hand I'd been dealt. But, no!

I found myself copying all the other people in business. Most people wore blue collared shirts, a tie, some chinos and smart black shoes. I assumed that this was 'the way business people dressed', so I wore the same. Nobody noticed me. Business was hard. My confidence sucked.

It wasn't until my early thirties when I got married, and my first little one arrived on the scene, and I realised that people weren't buying 'what' I was selling. They certainly weren't buying the collared shirt, bland colours and the shiny shoes. They were buying me.

This big 'aha' moment was the catalyst which led to me being bold and creating my own image. I'm a surfer not a city slicker and it was time my image reflected that.

Something surprising happened: A tribe started formed around me and my brand. People identify with my unique image; they feel empowered by it and want to see what this Robin Waite guy is all about.

Best of all no-one ever judges me for wearing Saltrock T's to work. It has brought colour back into my life, I feel comfortable in my new skin, I feel fearless. So fearless, in fact, that I have launched a T-Shirt range to reflect my own unique brand, image and identity.

A far cry from that little boy in the red cords. I am recognised for who I truly am.

It's an honour and a huge complement, from Berith, to be invited to write the foreword for *Define your signature style - Be recognised for who you are.*

Berith has gifted you this amazing story in her own unique and incredibly generous style. Prepare to have your eyes, and wardrobe doors opened and see yourself for who you truly are too.

Robin Waite
Founder, Fearless Business and bestselling author of
Online Business Startup and *Take Your Shot*

INTRODUCTION

Many factors are involved, making you the person you are today. Not just how you communicate or the way you dress, but also what you have learned: who you spend your time with and how you decide on what's important in your life.

Define your signature style - Be recognised for who you are is the story about Rose, her chance meeting with Elena and how she became inspired to embark on a journey to find her confidence in what to wear – thereby creating a signature style that reflected her core values and beliefs.

It soon transpires that, for many years, she has tried to be someone else. Copying and dressing according to what she thought people wanted her to look like. To blend in rather than stand out. Plus, it was clear that she had let herself go. As you will find out – when it comes to what to wear, she used to be one confused professional woman.

Rose's journey is based on my past experiences working with more than 100 professional women internationally; women who more than anything wanted to make their mornings easier - knowing what to wear and to claim their place in life with confidence.

I want to share this story with you, to save you the hassle of facing the same challenges, thus allowing you to grow in confidence without being discouraged or confused.

As you read on, I will share with you some of the tools that I use with a few pointers for you to follow. It won't be possible for me to share everything but it should give you a great starting point and an indication of how and where to find inspiration.

Even though my background is in fashion and beauty, I'm more passionate about portraying the actual person than the latest fashion. The truth is that I love people in the same way that I love fabrics – for having a personality and life of their own.

I know that your values and your dreams will differ from mine, and that's how it should be. And I hope that *Define your signature style – Be recognised for who you are* inspires you to take action, re-evaluate your personal style, focus on your true values and move you towards your goals.

What I have noticed is that we all have one thing in common - A survival instinct and a main purpose to explore the meaning of life and to understand who God intended us to be.
This is why this book is not about the latest fashion but about how you can give yourself permission to define who you are meant to be – and how to dress accordingly.

I do not have all the answers, there are many image consultants, stylist and brand experts who will give you excellent advice. The way I work, which is partly shared in this book, is a formula that does make a difference beyond a one-session experience in a studio.

So why do I focus on clothes when what's inside our hearts is far more important?

Clothes are part of our body language. Each garment will govern how we move and carry ourselves. One outfit can complete us and make us feel invincible, and others can make us feel like we are aliens forced to belong in an environment that doesn't feel authentic to who we are.

It's not just our heart, our values and beliefs that dictates our confidence level; we also need a clear vision, spiced with belief, to help us see where we are going.

As the purposeful being that YOU are, YOU have the power to move towards YOUR goals; no-one else can do this for you. But there are people around you who can give you inspiration and confidence to move with you in the right direction: to encourage and support you to become awesome with sincere integrity. It's up to you to choose wisely who these people should be, as well as who you wish people to remember you as.

I pray and hope that this book is the inspiration that you have been looking for when it comes to knowing what to wear; gaining more confidence; creating a signature style; and, defining who you truly are.

Enjoy and be inspired!

Benith

p.s. Make *Define your signature style - Be recognised for who you are* your book: Use any blank pages and margins for writing down thoughts and question that you want to ask me when we meet for your **complimentary** Style Audit.

"Knowing yourself is the beginning of all wisdom."

Aristotle

A Wise Decision

Really, is it really time to get up? It feels as if I've hardly slept, and today of all days. I must clinch that contract. I know I'm the right person to take the organisation to the next level of success. I've been praying for this opportunity for over a year. They told me that they love my proposal and today I have my chance to excel as we are meeting face-to-face.

Leaving my bed and heading for the bathroom I'm wondering if what I have chosen to wear would be appropriate. What did I decide on wearing in the end?

Really? It looked so nice last night, but now I'm not sure. Look at the bobbles around the armholes, and the fading colours around the neckline. The whole outfit is looking tired. Just like me... *What's happened to me?* I used to look so polished and put together. I used to love getting dressed. Even Toby is staring to comment on what I'm wearing, calling me second-hand Rose.

Well, he just doesn't get it, I'm bored running the home on my own, tired from writing proposals and disheartened that I'm not using my skills within an organisation, and it doesn't help that he's away most weeks, plus there is no reason for getting dressed up any more.

So ... what shall I wear? I want to be true to me. *Does it have to be so difficult?*

After taking a shower and moving towards my wardrobe with nothing else but a towel wrapped around my head, I reach for the doors, and I feel apprehension. What if I choose the wrong outfit? How do I know what's right? Feeling the butterflies flitting in my stomach I start to feel nauseous.

Before Andrew was born, I used to be so confident in my body, knowing exactly what looked best on me. Now I'm lost. *I just want to know what to wear and who stole my confidence?*

Taking a quick glance inside my wardrobe I see items hanging squashed together in a neat row. *Neat, that's me.* But everything is so cluttered when it comes to patterns, colours, textures and styles. How on earth can I find anything and where do I start? I really must stop buying things I don't need... I haven't got a clue what suits me any more ...

Ten minutes later I find a great dress which I know will enhance my best features. I always receive some fantastic positive comments when I wear it. *Why didn't I lay this one out last night?*

As I put it on, I realise that it's too small. I can't do the zip up. *Did I shrink it in the wash or have a gained in weight?* No time to ponder. Let's find something else.

Wearing my anorak over a classic navy dress and laden down with too many bags containing everything that I might need, including spare tights, I found my seat on the train.

As the train arrived at the station, I had plenty of time to spare before my interview. I noticed a little café on the other side of the street. *I'm going to treat myself to a coffee.* Well and truly inside and away from the rain, I found a spare table in a corner and just as I was about to sit down, I heard a familiar voice call my name.

"Rose! It is you!" I turned around and there was Elena, with a friendly smile on her face, looking so put together, thus making me feel like a bag lady. We've worked together on several projects in the past and used to get on very well. We had lost contact after her daughter had been born. It must have been at least 14 years ago, and now it was as if we had never been apart. We embraced and started filling in the gaps.

"It's so lovely seeing you again! Tell me, how is everyone and what are you doing here, in this area?" she asked. I explained that we were all well, that I had started my own consultancy business after gaining a MSc in Ecological

Economics three years before, and that I was off in half an hour to pitch to a marketing company not far from away.

She smiled and asked the name, and when I told her she was grinning. "What a coincidence! That's the company I'm currently working with. Not much longer though as I'm off to China in a few months' time."

Her smile subsided as she quickly glanced at what I was wearing, which made me feel uncomfortable - I could sense that she was aware of my reaction. "I'm sorry, I didn't mean to disarm you, it's just... I know what Abbi is going to think when you walk in wearing that rain coat. May I suggest something that may help you today?"

I nodded, and she continues.

"Leave you anorak and walk in without it. That way they will remember you for looking healthy, not worn out."

My anorak... It doesn't surprise me you think it's drab, Toby hates it, and he can't for his life understand why I like wearing it. I like the colour and it is rain proof, that's about it.

I reassured her that I appreciated her honesty and that I would visit my local charity shop to see what they had on offer. "What's wrong with a new coat?", asked Elena.

I explained. *I watched this program about the global cost of fashion last autumn. I was horrified and vowed to do my best purchasing clothes that didn't cost the earth. Plus, shopping at charity shops doesn't bother me.*

"I can hear your passion, which is so important, but I know that a tidy appearance is appreciated and will be expected. After all, they are known for producing high quality. Your dress is beautiful and looks in line with their core values, but your anorak…"

I could see and feel the sincerity in her voice when she spoke next. "Don't take this the wrong way, but I think you would benefit from seeing a personal stylist."

Elena, I've been there. It's no use. I paid hundreds of pounds to have my colours analysed a few years back and my style was nit-picked. It left me feeling deflated rather than confident.

"I know what you mean. It all depends on who you are working with. A little bit like you being excellent at what you do and knowing full well that there will be someone out there, claiming to be just as good though not delivering to the same high standard and integrity as what you have to offer. That's why third-party validation is valuable. You trust me, don't you?

Yes, I trust you, and you are right!

Elena continued, "You know what? I think you should contact Bridget. She's more of a personal brand stylist than an image consultant and I think the two of you will get on really well. She is a strong advocate for quality and integrity. I think she is involved in her church, just like you." She took out a card from her bag and wrote down a number "Here's her number. Call her!"

I looked down and saw that she'd written Bridget's number on her personal business card. I looked up and smiled. I didn't want to sound ungrateful, so I told her that I would consider giving Bridget a call. *I'll definitely contact her if I don't get this contract, and I'll let you know the outcome.*

The pitch went relatively well. A couple of awkward incidents relating to my posture more than anything. My communication was spot on but I was fidgeting. Playing with my hem and stroking the fabric in an attempt to flatten some creases that wouldn't go away. Perhaps I'm too self-conscious? Working with this company had been my goal for five years. Now I just had to wait. They said they would let me know early next week.

On the train back I thought of the chance encounter meeting Elena. I promised myself that no matter what, contract or no contract, I would start working towards a more polished me.

I will contact Bridget first thing tomorrow morning.

"Be patient with yourself. Self-growth is tender; it's holy ground. There's no greater investment."

Stephen Covey

Know Thyself

Putting the book down, I took a deep breath filling my lungs and then slowly exhale. It's not often I read a book with so much wisdom. I've learned so much about myself, how to apply gratitude and affirmation in to my daily life - filling my heart with a hope for the future. *'The Power of I am' by Joel Osteen - what a wonderful book and, a great title too!*

Searching in my purse for the name and number that Elena had given me I smiled. Just meeting her, after so many years, it felt as if we'd never been apart. She is a good friend; I mean, only a good friend can lift you up whilst giving such sincere advice face-to-face. Funny though, I didn't feel hurt by what she said about my image. She had ignited a new flame in my being. She'd given me permission to explore finding my authentic image and style.

As I picked up my purple Bullet Journal to check on yesterday's happenings, and to claim a new day, I noticed that I'd created a rather nice border around Bridget's name and phone number. Subconsciously I must have felt drawn to the idea of stepping out of my confused comfort zone, even though I'd never met her.

Tapping her number into my phone I began writing her a personal message.

Hi Bridget, I've been given your number from Elena Jusuf and she believes you can help me. She mentioned that you work with women who wish to find their signature style. This sounds like something I could benefit from, but I'm not sure. I've already had my colours and style done, so I would like to know what makes you different from your competitors?

Look forward hearing from you.

Warmest, Rose.

Checking the other notes from yesterday I noticed a scribble next to Bridget's name that said "China? Philippines?" Now I remembered, Elena mentioning that Bridget was currently abroad in the far east. China or Philippines? *Never mind. I'm sure she'll get back to me in due course.*

Leaving my phone safely away from what I needed to focus on without being disturbed by bleeps and notifications, I embarked on writing a new proposal. Finishing the outline, I was ready to take a break at 11, and out of habit I reached for my phone before putting the kettle on. I had several messages to check through, and one was from Bridget.

"Hi Rose, thank you for reaching out. I'm currently in the Philippines and will return this Saturday. Perhaps we could meet up virtually the following week? It's easy to book a session that suits your diary and there's no obligation to purchase anything. Just click on the link which will direct you to my booking platform.

Meanwhile, and if you are ready to find your confidence score, I recommend that you take the Confidence Calculator assessment. At the end you will find out how congruent you are between the three brand pillars that are representing your signature style – your personal brand.

Should you wish to work with me, defining your image, we will ensure these are balanced.

Once again, thank you for getting in touch.

Regards, Bridget."

That was a nice response. No obligation... brand pillars...? *Well, I'm ready to find my authentic image, so let's take the first step and see where it takes me.* Finding my confidence level sounded very interesting.

The assessment only took me seven minutes and when I had finished, I received an email highlighting the total score of 78 plus an invitation to book the Style Audit. There was also a promise of something else to follow within 48 hours. *Now I'm curious.*

I decided to book the following Tuesday at 2pm. That way I would have found out if I'd been offered the consultancy role or not. If I didn't get it, I would know that it was due to my overall confidence in my personal image. If I did get it... well, I would just have to embrace the fact that I was a work in progress and that I wanted more opportunities to grow in confidence.

Looking back on my previous attempts to find my image, I knew I had felt intimidated and unsure if I was doing the right thing. There was so much I had to change and maintain. I just couldn't keep up with it all.

The following Saturday, when Toby and I were walking beside the river, catching up with life's ups and downs we checked in with present and future plans. He'd been away for a couple of weeks and, as always, our time together was precious. His plans for that day were straightforward, to scuba dive with Andrew in the afternoon and take me out for a meal that evening.

He asked me about my week and what it had been like and I shared how and where I'd bumped into Elena, how well she looked and that she gently had suggested that I should invest some time and money on my image.

He smiled "I'm delighted to hear that you met Elena." He paused and continued. "I think she's right; you deserve to find your confidence. So, have you decided on what to do about it?

Elena recommended someone. Her name is Bridget and she's some kind of Brand Stylist. Not sure exactly what the difference is compared to an image consultant, but I trust Elena's recommendation. By the way, she looked younger than she did 14 years ago. Whatever she is doing, I want some of that!

Toby's grin was wider now and I could see that he was excited about something.

"If it's the same Bridget that spoke at a business conference in Shanghai two years ago, I know you will get on well. When I heard her sincere passion, I was seriously thinking about treating you to work with her, but I chickened out."

Feeling a little bit alarmed and looking at him suspiciously, I asked him why he didn't do it or at least tell me about this 'Bridget' before.

"Well, I wasn't sure if I would hurt your feelings giving you such a personal prompt. I mean, you may have been insulted, and I didn't, and still don't, want to hurt your feelings, as I know that you are not as confident as you used to be. I have been praying that a light bulb moment would happen for you to decide for yourself." He paused then continued with a question. "Am I right to think that meeting Elena was a divine appointment for you?"

Yes, I responded with a smirk. *You know me all too well.*

"So, what's your next step?"

I hesitated before I answered. *I've got a virtual consultation with Bridget this coming Tuesday and I'll take it from there.* He stopped in his tracks and turned to me whilst looking me straight in the eye.

"I'd like to sponsor you." Now it was my turn to stop in my tracks and with a confident voice letting him know that I needed to do this for me - Invest my time and money in finding my confident style. Being true to me.

Walking back home, after we had enjoyed a nice hearty brunch at our favourite café, I was thinking about the answers to the assessment Bridget had sent me. I hadn't looked at it properly as I wanted to do this when I was on my own.

Squeezing all their gear into the back of the BMW i3, Toby and Andrew set off for their adventure. They'd be gone a couple of hours at least, which would give me plenty of time to really study the answers to the assessment.

As soon as I knew they were gone, I made myself a hot drink, opened up the balcony doors and sat down in my favourite chair with a blanket over my legs. The air was fresh and I took in my favourite view. The scent from the Hyacinths, that had just started to emerge, was so uplifting and the sound from the blackbird singing...

Spring! My favourite time of the year.

"It's no use going back to yesterday, because I was a different person then."

Alice in Wonderland

A True Representation

I always dreamt about living by the sea, but Toby and I came to the conclusion that as I predominantly work from home, I would never get anything done. Also, there are fewer seagulls and tourists further inland, so this is the perfect spot. An inspirational office at home, with a sea view, and with easy access to the shore should we need it.

As I was reading through what Bridget had revealed, I could clearly see that her 'Confidence Calculator' was spot on. The assessment showed three pillars in various heights. The tallest represented my business. She'd put a personal note saying that she was curious to find out what I could do for her business. *Interesting...* I would add that thought to my Bullet Journal to make sure I'd follow up when appropriate.

One of the other pillars represented my purpose in the form of my ideal client. The comment here was that I was clear on who needed me. Which was great, and then there was another comment saying that I most likely needed to fine-tune and focus on who I really wanted to work with, because, as Bridget had put it – I was trying to be everything to everyone.

The third pillar was the shortest, and represented my confidence in who I was when representing my business.

Bridget was posing the question that perhaps there had been a confidence knock somewhere along the line, and that maybe additional business or sales focused coaching would benefit me.

My past... I remember a couple of incidents. Once when I was called up on stage, ad hoc, to participate in a sketch that two of my school friends were presenting. I remember that I was shy and unsure but I that I trusted them, so I obliged. At the end they made me look and feel a total fool. I'm not sure if I cried but it still makes me uneasy just thinking about it. I was seven years old and if I'm asked without warning to participate, I freeze. I hate being put on the spot. How sad, so trivial and so long ago yet it had left a scar. The second incident, which actually was before the 'on stage' humiliation, was when I was asked to 'go home' by a group of friends because they didn't want to play with me. I obliged, but I can still feel the sadness within me, feeling rejected and unwanted. I think this is when I stopped asking to be involved, waiting to be invited and learning to enjoy my own company. Anyhow... that was so long ago. I wondered if this had defined me?

Bridget's final comment and recommendation for me was to consider the Confidence Creator program, which she said would reveal and help me create habits and maintain my authentic personal style.

I noticed that there was a direct link at the bottom of the email. Clicking on it I found myself on Bridget's website. The site itself was basic, just a few pages, but all the necessary information was there, including a link should I want to do the assessment again.

Getting acquainted with the website, reading about her and looking at the three different services that she provided, I could see that the Confidence Creator was the most expensive, and she was recommending to do it over 90 days.

Wow! Not a quick fix then!

Deep in thought, I could hear a car approach on our gravelled driveway. I stood up and leaned over the railing and wondered who it could be. It was Elena, and as she stepped out, she waved and called out.

"Is this a bad time? I was in the neighbourhood."

I waved back and replied that it was perfect timing and invited her to come in for a drink.

Pulling out another chair and a blanket, she joined me on the balcony. Making herself comfortable she asked me if I had been in touch with Bridget.

I told her that I had contacted Bridget the previous Wednesday, and that I'd had the assessment score come through the other day with some very clear points to ponder.

"Assessment? That sounds as if she has developed her service even further. Tell me, what have you found out?"

I shared the score with Elena explaining that the three pillars exposed my values as being strong but that my vision was a bit wobbly due to not knowing my purpose; as was my confidence in representing myself.

"Values and vision?"

I reached for my laptop to show her what the assessment had revealed.

"This is wonderful!" She exclaimed. "Bridget is drawing attention to the importance of having a strong foundation with three similar pillars to support your vision. I love it!"

Yes, and as you can see, my pillars are uneven. My strength is in my knowledge and the love for my business, but when it comes to understanding my purpose and who my ideal client is and who I am to them... I'm not congruent.

"I wouldn't worry too much. There is room for improvement. I know Bridget will find the best solution for you. She will inspire you to embrace your personal self-discovery journey - perhaps not in the same capacity as what you are used to, but I know the two of you speak a similar language."

It started to get dark and as I glanced at my watch, I knew that Toby and Andrew would be back from their dive soon, which meant that I needed to get myself ready for our date-night. Folding up the blankets and putting the chairs safely away from the weather, Elena and I walked back into the open plan living area whilst planning our next catch up.

"Let me know how you get on with Bridget. What you've shared with me now has brought back some very fond memories and The Confidence Calculator has made me curious. I think I need to take it myself."

Her comment surprised me and I asked her. *Why would you do the assessment?*

"It's good to have a reality check now and then, don't you think? Plus, I need to update a few items in my wardrobe and I think the 'Polish' service would work wonders."

Without knowing why, I nodded. But Elena sounded confident. "See you Wednesday." she said as she gave me a hug before driving away.

As I stood there, looking at all the clothes in my wardrobe, I felt disheartened and unable to see anything that I actually wanted to wear. I could hear 'the boys' return from their adventure. Grabbing hold of my favourite trousers, a jersey top and a little cardigan, I got dressed to hear what they had found below the water's edge.

"Dream and give yourself permission to envision a YOU that you chose to be."

Joy Page

Permission to Change

Five minutes to go … I clicked on the link to attend our meeting and there she was, waiting for me.

"Hi Rose! Lovely meeting you face to face. How was your weekend?"

I shared how much I had enjoyed my weekend being with my husband, studying and sharing the outcome of the assessment with Elena. I also mentioned that I was excited, though a little bit hesitant about this whole experience.

"Why do you think this is?"

I really don't know, but perhaps it's something to do with past experiences. Not knowing what to expect, plus having had my colours and style analysed a few years back I'm a little bit sceptical, perhaps even cynical. But Elena promised that you work differently from most. Can you expand on what the difference is?

"Of course, I have a formula that focuses on the client rather than the latest fashion. I ensure it's tailored to your needs."

So, nothing to do with colour and style?

"Definitely something to do with both, but not the main purpose. Those are tools for you and I to use when it comes to defining your best and most attractive style. Understanding what colours suits you will be a great help and a confidence boost when we put your capsule wardrobe together. The aim is for us to create a style that's authentic to you - your signature."

That sounded promising, but even so. *Do I really need to have my colours done and style analysed again?*

"It would help me if I could understand your colours better. That way I can explain and show you in detail why certain colours work best on you and which ones to avoid. The online style assessment is a little bit of fun, especially if you wish to attract a new audience and woo your ideal client before you open your mouth."

I do wish to attract bigger and better clients, but more importantly, I want that contract. I shared this with Bridget, and added:

I've been asked back next week to do a presentation for the board of directors. This time I want to look and behave confidently. No fidgeting.

"Congratulations and well done! So, what does 'no fidgeting' look like to you?"

Good posture I suppose. Eye contact and clothes that fit well.

"That's all in the preparation. And I'm sure you know that already?"

Yes. I sighed. *I'm great at preparing, I just need to know the foundational truths behind the prep and then it's relatively easy.*

"Rose, I need to ask one important question…What are you hoping for?"

I paused, took a deep breath (I'd been dreading this question) and as I exhaled, I answered her question in one long breath. *I really don't know what I'm hoping for apart from feeling more confident in what to wear.*

I took a lighter breath and continued. *I tend to panic before I present to a large corporation. They all seem so polished, which is good, but I always feel a mess. I suppose knowing what to wear would be valuable, without compromising on my values.*

"Can you expand on what you think your values are?"

I shared that I valued integrity as well as creativity; that I liked to follow a good system, and that my aim was to excel beyond expectations. Plus, to care for the environment was top of my agenda.

She nodded, and replied with one short sentence. "I hear you."

Then she paused before continuing. "You are passionate and it would be good to unleash some of this fire within you in, without being pretentious. Would you like to find out how to achieve this?"

Yes! When can we start?

"As soon as you have appointed me to coach you. We need to decide on a mutual date and I need to understand a little bit more about who you are, the work you do, and what makes you different from your competition."

Now?

"If you don't mind."

I shared with her how I came to be involved in environmental economics; what I felt my gift was; my love and passion for sustainability; and why I believed that every company as well as individual needed to adopt a different attitude in how we live and what we love.

Bridget replied. "I love that. Have you tried wearing your passion?"

I thought I did. I mean, I shop in second hand shops and I like to think I dress in a way that's approachable.

"So, what do you think is happening?"

I pondered for a couple of second and replied with a smile.

That's what I would like you to show me.

"That's what I was hoping you would say. But first of all, you need to give yourself permission to let go as well as move forward. Starting this self-discovery adventure will change some aspects of how people see you and you need to be totally sure that you are ready to explore and learn. You need to invite me to be part of your journey. But I think you have verbalised this already. Am I right?"

I have!

Bridget continued explaining that the program could be a choice of either 30 or 90 days. All depending on how committed I was to do the assignments.

Assignments... *You won't be doing this for me?*

"We will be doing this together. When I first started working as an image consultant it was all about me doing everything for my clients. Colour analysis, filling in the style questionnaire, weeding wardrobes, taking pictures, finding outfits... Of course, I can do all this for you, but I know that you won't remember what to do when I leave you to it. Maintaining your wardrobe and confidence is key for nailing your signature style. It takes time creating a new habit."

"I'm not sure if I can do this in 30 days... all depending on getting the contract or not. Perhaps 90 days is more feasible. How many hours shall I allocate per week?"

"You decide and I'll hold you accountable." She continued. "Early on, you need to do the work, to assess what you already have. Half way through, week 6ish, I will start compiling your capsule wardrobe; create specific outfits, followed by putting together a shopping list according to your purpose, core values and vision. When it comes to how much time to allocate, it depends on the assignment, but I recommend that you commit one hour on top of each consultation. That's likely to be at least one hour per week over a period of 12 weeks."

I agreed that I could commit to this.

Before confirming our next session, she asked me about my online presence. How active I was and how much work I accumulated via social media, especially LinkedIn.

I told her that I was plodding along though wasn't active as such. Then she asked about Networking groups and how many I attended each month.

'On average, two. I find some of them intimidating as I don't know who's going to be there or what to wear.'

Taking down notes, she asked me if I knew what good friends, thought of me. Why they liked to be with me.

I can't speak for everyone. I'm loyal, a calm influence but I can come across as being reserved.

"Do you see yourself as reserved and do you mind?"

I don't mind, but I know that inside of me there is a fire burning and a Goddess waiting to emerge.

It surprised me how easy it was to share personal feelings with Bridget. I found myself answering without hesitation.

She looked up as she was taking notes. "Thank you for sharing." She said. "I know how you feel and you are not alone. Here's the thing - it starts with you wanting more, to be better. So, if you want to be more when it comes to how you represent yourself in what you wear - now is your time to start being more.

She put her pen down and promised that she would be forwarding my personalised program when everything was confirmed.

"After you've forwarded the forms, check your email for instructions on how we will share various assignments. Also, let's allocate Tuesdays as our day and Mondays as your deadline. How does that sound?"

Sounds great!

"It is never too late to be who you might have been."

George Eliot

Never Too Late

As soon as I had paid my first instalment, Bridget sent me an email with the program outline and an explanation of what I needed to focus on next.

"Hi Rose, thank you for returning the signed contract and your payment. I'm delighted to be your co-pilot on this journey – defining your signature style.

Your first assignment is to nail your vision. You decide if you want to do this actually by using paper, scissors and glue; or digitally. Either way, you need to share the final picture with me. When you go about creating your vision board, make sure to include images that represents where you wish to be in five years' time. It doesn't have to be exactly a five-year plan. Just make sure it's what you wish to experience in the future – Then focus on the following seven vision points:

- Where you wish to live
- How you wish to travel
- What you wish to be wearing/ your style
- What your ideal client looks like
- Where you would spend your vacation
- What you want your business to look like
- What makes you truly happy – your passion"

She also invited me to a WhatsApp group, just for the two of us. Where images as well as assessments were to be shared. Apparently, we would be using another app towards the end, but she said that I didn't have to worry about this until half way through. It was some sort of photo sharing 'cloud' app. *I'm intrigued.*

As it was, I didn't really engage on WhatsApp, I had a profile, though I didn't do much with it. But she did say that unless she found a better way to communicate, FB was the easiest for both of us to access... I promised to give it a go.

Looking at my scheduled plan for that day, I decided to work until lunch time, putting another proposal together, and then give myself an hour over lunch focusing on creating my vision board. Subconsciously I'd already started the process – visualising my future in pictures. I always worked towards my goals by using mind maps, but now I was to add pictures, and quotes. *Very creative.*

At 10 am I gave up on the proposal. I just couldn't focus. My heart was longing to start the creative visualisation. So, instead of being in front of my screen, I decided to stop fighting and embrace the creativity process until Lunch break.

Taking a pile of old magazines out of my office I laid them out on the kitchen table – National Geographic, The

Economist, Psychologies, DIVE. *I'm sure there must be something suitable here.*

There we are! I'd found the perfect image to represent what I wanted my business to look like - two images in fact, super imposed. It was me, lifting up a smiling earth. This image also reflected what I visualised my home life to be like in five years - green, clean, happy and thriving. In some ways it already was. It was me that needed some uplifting.

Perhaps I was an idealist? But, the future for our world wasn't that bright, and I was applying positivity here. This is what I wanted: a happy life and a happy earth, so I'd be focusing on the positives. It was my vision after all and I liked to be recognised for having these values in place.

As I stood up, stretching my back, whilst looking at my finished assignment, I smiled. This was me - tomorrow, and for the future. I was sure I'd be ready to embrace the changes. At least, now I knew what I wanted. I had a much clearer vision.

Looking out of the window, I could see that clouds were threatening rain, and as I had 30 minutes to spare before lunch, I decided to catch some fresh air. Looking at my anorak with a wry smile, I put it on and headed for the valley across the road. It had been an odd winter; the fields reflected an eerie shade of grey. Some rain, and sunshine, would be very welcome.

I found a sheltered spot overlooking the lower field. Apart from the cacophony of crows gathering in a tree nearby everything was still. I lifted my face towards the sky and as I closed my eyes, I could feel a drop of rain touch my cheek.

Feeing hopeful, I started to find a new confidence emerge. I'd forgotten what it felt like knowing for sure who I was and what I wanted. No matter what happened, getting this contract or not, I'd made a contract with myself to discover me, and to wear my confidence.

Empowered and optimistic, even though the rain was coming down heavily by now, I didn't hurry. I just walked steadily back home with a feeling that a positive change and cleansing process was about to happen.

As soon as I was back inside and dried off, I took a picture of my vision board and shared it with Bridget, as per her request. When I looked at my post, it felt like a solid confirmation. I had given myself permission, not just to work on my image but also to dream, to be certain of what I couldn't see – to have hope and a future.

I think someone once referred to it as having faith…

"Being honest may not get you a lot of friends but it'll always get you the right ones."

John Lennon

The Honest Truth

Elena was sitting by the window. I waved at her and she smiled and waved back. We decided last time we met to hook up for a bite to eat after I had finished my second interview.

"How did you feel it went?" She asked.

Assuring her that I didn't fidget once, I sat down with a combined sigh of relief and a hearty smile on my lips.

"I'm so pleased for you. You look more confident today than the last time I saw you. More composed. I think that's a good sign. When will you find out? "

I told her that the interview, which was more of a presentation, went very well and that I felt in control of the situation.

I should be hearing something by the end of this week. Having had a chance to put my vison in place and sharing the image with Bridget has given me a great confidence boost.

I told her that, according to Bridget, I was now ready to start working on my aspired style. A style that would reflect and compliment my vision as well as my values. *She's given me another assessment – The Style Quest.*

"It's fun and light hearted. I think you will like it."

I looked Elena straight in the eye. *So far, I'm loving this journey. It's the same feeling I had when I first fell in love with Toby. Love and lust. Funny though, I am starting to feel more lust towards him.* We started to giggle when we realise what I've just proclaimed.

"Steady!" Elena giggled. "What an amazing journey you are embarking on. I remember mine like it was yesterday. You just wait until you get to understand what fabrics work best for you, and patterns… and how to put outfits together from your capsule wardrobe. Nothing is going to stop you. You will love YOU and lust for Toby even more!"

By now we were belly laughing. Just the thought, lusting afresh for a man, my man, because I was falling in love with myself. I didn't mind this at all, as long as Toby didn't mind the change in me.

Elena, I've heard stories that some marriages break up due to a drastic change in one person becoming more self-confident. Is this what happened to you and Paul?

"No, he left me five years ago, for a younger model. I felt so hurt but it spurred me on to take a good look at what I wanted out of life, which prompted me to evaluate my self-image. I soon realised that it wasn't just the way I looked. He would probably have left me somewhere down the line anyway. He didn't love me."

She looked directly at me and with serenity in her eyes. "I wouldn't worry about Toby. You two have a good honest relationship going... don't you? "

She was totally right, after all, it was Toby who first heard of Bridget and thought of me.

Yes, we do have a good relationship going. And he's behind me on this journey. He even offered to sponsor me.

"You declined?"

Yes, I need to invest in this for me, with my own capital.

Elena smiled and continued. "As you are starting to see the gaps, finding 'you', you may need it to purchase new clothes."

That's true, but my clothes just need to work. I really don't care if they are new or old, as long as they represent me in a professional and attractive way; clothes that suits me well.

"I'm with you, and the three of you will make it work."

Did I hear this correctly? *The three of us... what do you mean?*

"Well, Toby is part of you, and Bridget, well she's your coach and mentor. Just in case there is a rapid change in you, Toby might need to be part of this journey. Invite him. Share with him how you feel and what you are experiencing. He can always decline, though I have a feeling he won't."

Gosh, I'd never thought of that and I promised myself to ask Toby and invite him to be part of what I was learning about myself.

Elena continued with another question. "By the way, have you found your core value points yet?"

Not yet. But Bridget did mention that I was to receive something in the post to help me find my three core values, and that we would use these three to establish my brand colours.

"Oh yes! It is a great exercise. As soon as you know this you will be able to create solid marketing materials including adverts, business cards and your website. And, you will be able to tie at least one colour in with what you are wearing – making it your signature colour."

That sounded absolutely awesome, and it prompted me to ask Elena if hers, by any chance, was Teal? I had noticed that teal was a main colour on her business card and that she always wore a teal scarf – being around her neck or tied to her bag.

"Yes, Teal is one of my colours. It's definitely the one I love wearing the most. The other two - Purple and Gold are lovely too, but I don't feel as great wearing those."

Now I was intrigued. *Teal, Purple and Gold... I wouldn't mind any of those colours.*

"Apparently Gold doesn't suit my complexion, and Purple, even though it's a good colour on me, it doesn't make me happy. So, I avoid wearing those two."

You know what? I'm really looking forward finding mine.

"I'm looking forward to hearing all about it."

As we embraced, we promised to compare notes and meet again the following week.

"Open your arms to change but don't let go of your values."

Dalai Lama

With Open Arms

The past three weeks had flown by. Not only did I enjoy focusing on what I wanted out of life and whom to be remembered as, but I also revelled in my new-found confidence.

The day after having lunch with Elena, I received a package in the post from Bridget.

As I opened the small padded envelope, I was surprised to see what looked like a pack of playing cards. They had numbers and letters like an ordinary pack, but written on them were different sets of 'value words.' Helen Harrison, the author and creator of these, had included eight different exercises that would help me gain a clear understanding what my personal as well as corporate core values were.

Looking through the cards, after reading an encouraging note from Bridget, I started with exercise number 1 – 'What are your values?'

I found a dozen words that resonated with my career and another 20 relating to my personal development.

When I shared these with Bridget, asking for advice, she replied, "For you, out of all these, what are your three strongest values, the ones you would never compromise on?"

I replied that Harmony, Compassion and Clarity were my three but that I had another couple that were possible.

She encouraged me to ponder on these and recommended that I do the first exercise again. Then she invited me to meet face to face the following day. "It's important that we get this right" she said.

When we met, I confirmed that I hadn't changed my mind and she was happy that my values were that strong. Then she said to focus on my ideal client. As we did this together, I realized that when it came to it, I struggled to pinpoint their values. I knew what they looked like and where they lived, sort of, but value words? No.

"As soon as you know who they are, inside out, you will be able to create a much stronger brand."

It took 20 minutes before we settled on my Avatar's core values - Strength, Security and Clarity. *That means that we have one great value point in common – Clarity.*

"The other two gives us a great indicator how we can work towards a more successful brand for you. I don't want you to be pretentious, just aware what it is your ideal client is attracted to in you."

She continued. "I'm already starting to see the gap between your values and your vision. And to be honest, the gap isn't that big."

Fab, so, there is still hope?

"Absolutely, plenty of hope. I'm very honoured to be with you on this journey. If it helps, I recommended that you book a session with a business coach or marketeer who understands the importance of using the right words to reach your audience."

She gave me two names that she thought would suit my specific needs and encouraged me to align with my instinct, to contact both and decide who to work with after I'd talked to each one.

"Do you feel ready for your next assignment?"

Yep, I'm ready. I replied.

"This is relatively easy, but first you must promise me not to cheat. Okay?"

Okay, what do you want me to do?

Bridget asked me to go straight to my wardrobe, open it up and take a picture of all my clothes in it. "No cheating!" She said. "Take a picture of what it looks like without you taking anything away."

She explained that she wanted to see the true me, to compare the 'Style Quest' with the actual clothes, and apparently, the way I arrange my wardrobe indicates how congruent my style personality actually was.

-

The following day, and with some apprehension, I opened up my wardrobe and took three pictures. One image of what it looked like with the doors fully opened, another of what was hiding on the floor below and a third picture of what I had in the overhead cupboard.

When I shared these three images, I also admitted that I had boxes underneath my bed, a second wardrobe in the spare bedroom and two chests of drawers full of a mixed bunch of items, and most likely something lingering in the attic too.

In her reply, she told me that she could see that I like to keep things in order and that I probably had enough clothes to open my own charity shop.

"How do you feel when you open up your wardrobe?" she asked.

Bewildered and lost. I replied.

"That's understandable. Would you like to hear my observation?"

Absolutely.

"Excellent. Let's discuss this tomorrow at our scheduled time and we'll go over it then."

I couldn't wait to hear her verdict. Soon after we finished our session, she posted a diagram in our hub explaining my brand colours according to my values.

Evidently, the colour representing harmony was Green; Compassion was represented by Pink; and Clarity was blue.

Bridget said that it would make sense to choose Teal as my main brand color, and perhaps pink as my accent.

She explained: "Teal is a combination of blue and green and it's also a neutral colour – a hue that suits everyone. However, we need to know how much brightness you can take next to your face. You are your best marketing tool – a walking talking bill board! So, wearing your brand colours would make sense. A great way in making your core values official."

I love Teal but I'm not sure about Pink...

"You don't have to wear pink all over. Just an accent here and there. Nail varnish or lipstick; a watch strap; or perhaps a wallet ... Make it yours. Claim it and have fun.

But wait with purchasing anything until we have finished our second module."

Nail varnish… No that won't happen. As it's plastic. But a purse or a bag. That excites me.

She smiled and replied. "Just make sure to be true to you and your brand values."

> "Education is the kindling of a flame, not the filling of a vessel."

Socrates

A Burning Desire

Bridget came straight to the point. "Having these many clothes, and I believe it's just the tip of the ice-berg, means that you are most likely holding on to items for one of the following two reasons:

1. You don't like to get rid of anything as your clothes are sentimental, or
2. You haven't got a clue what suits you which means you keep buying clothes but you feel guilty getting rid of anything, just in case.

Which of these two resonates with you?"

How sad! Both of these resonate with me. I don't know what suits me. I purchase outfits that I see in a window display. I bring them home after I tried them on but only wear them once as I realise that they don't feel right on me. I feel guilty for only wearing them once and pack them away. I get attached to old favourites and even though they no longer fit me and look dated and sad, I hold on to them because I can't throw anything away. Am I insane?

"No, Rose, you are not insane. Whilst men tend to buy gadgets, women have a tendency buying clothes for buying's sake - to fill a void." She continued. "Knowing what to look for and how to find a true bargain is a skill which you are about to learn. Old habit needs to be put to rest and a new habit need to be created."

She continued with a question. "What do you feel like doing right now?

Get rid of everything that's wrong.

"But how do you know what is wrong?"

I thought for a second, then answered. *I really don't know. This is why I have so much in my wardrobe, isn't it?*

"Most likely, but I'm sure you can start clearing some of the clutter today. Are you ready to get started?

Definitely!

"As soon as possible, remove everything you have hanging in your second wardrobe. You did admit you have a second wardrobe…which is brilliant, every woman should have two wardrobes. Make sure to clear the boxes under the bed. Our aim is to lighten the load. To tame your wardrobe, so to speak."

She continued. "You will use your second wardrobe as an interim storage space until it becomes your hibernation unit - A place where your best items from the previous season will be resting until next time.

Here's how you get started:

- Discard any item that is soiled, broken, sad or outright ugly (your discretion)
- Establish what items of clothing you love wearing and put these away until we are ready to analyse them
- If you can, and I recommend that you do, go through the boxes under your bed as well as the drawers and analyse each item in the same way
- If you are struggling to discard an item for sentimental reasons, then air it, fold it and store it in a dry place where there is absolutely no moisture in the air.

Can you see the benefit from doing this?"

I can! I have thought of doing this for a very long time but wasn't sure where to start. So... you said to keep my second wardrobe as a hibernation unit. Does that mean I'll be moving my clothes next season?

"Yes, moving your clothes from one area to another will ensure they get some extra airing, which will keep them fresh and in good health for longer. Providing that the hangers are suitable and moths have been kept at bay."

Right, that makes sense. So, how about the boxes? I have a feeling that what's hiding under my bed are clothes that I forgotten that I had.

"Can you remember what might be hiding there?"

Sorry, I haven't got a clue. It's likely to be Toby's stuff as well.

"Okay, that's possible. I suggest you take your own items out and leave Toby's. Then get rid of anything that doesn't serve you. Especially if it seen it's day.'

We continued talking about what to look for and how I would know what was worth keeping.

Before we finished our session, Bridget gave me my next assignment.

"I need you to take some more photos, and this time images of you. These need to be taken in day light, though not direct sunlight. Overcast is best."

She gave me instructions of what I needed to do and she highlighted the importance of being captured naturally, without makeup.

The following morning, whilst I was getting dressed and ready, I could hear Toby calling me from the landing, but I didn't catch what he was saying. Something to do with the guest bed room… *Oh Yes! I know.*

Walking in his direction, I replied. *It's my stuff. My discarded clothes. What are you doing in there anyway?*

"No reason, the door was open and I'm just surprised to see so many black sacks. Are they all doomed for the dump?"

I don't know yet. I'm just following Bridget's instruction to clear the clutter. The clothes on the bed are too nice to discard and the ones in the black sacks... I don't love them enough to keep, and some are just sad and worn out.

"There are five sacks! You mean you have been holding on to items that you really didn't like?"

I tried to smile, but it turned in to a grin. *I didn't even know I had kept it all. Sad, eh?*

"How do you feel about it? Getting rid of 'stuff'?"

Starting off it was hard, there are so many memories attached to some of these. Look at this! Do you remember the Moulin Rouge party and this corset that I wore?

Toby was grinning, "That corset is amazing. I remember struggling to unlace you... Did you end up wearing it to bed, all night?"

I did! Such great memory.

"It was a great evening, and night."

Hmmm... And now I have to decide what to do with it. What do you suggest? Keep it or discard it?

"What does Bridget say about it?"

I haven't mentioned it. She just said to put sentimental items away. So, I think I'll wrap it up and store it away, somewhere.

"Why don't you frame it?"

And, where do you suggest I display it? In my office?

Toby winked and smiled. "There is only one place to display it – our bedroom!"

Heh heh, I'll take that as confirmation that it is as sentimental to you as it is to me.

Glancing at my own reflexion in the bathroom mirror, I could hear Toby drive off in his car. It was going to be a great day - packed full of with getting to know the true me.

I removed the tripod from its bag and fastened my smart phone to it. Setting the timer for three seconds, I quickly positioned myself in front of the camera against a wall which I had first thought had good light. I was wrong. Taking a look at the image of me, I noticed heavy shadows playing on my face. And there wasn't enough clarity.

Moving the tripod and camera towards the balcony I did the same manoeuvre again. Clicked the timer, rushed to stand in front of the camera, smiled and checked the image.

After fifteen minutes, fiddling about with timer, position and pose, I found a place to stand where the light and reflection was acceptable. *That's better. No eyes closed in this one.*

When I had finished, I quickly, and without being too self-critical, posted the images in our group.

Bridget had told me that I would most likely have a eureka moment doing this assignment, and she was right. Studying my features, I noticed several points of interest.

- Eyes – grey blue with an added sparkle
- Complexion – could do with more colour
- Hair – medium brown and no need for hair dye
- Teeth – could do with some brightening
- Lips – kissable…
- Body – could do with some toning

I started to see me in a new light. *Not bad for 43.*

"Change is inevitable; Progress is optional."

Tony Robbins

A Work in Progress

The following Tuesday evening, Bridget and I had our usual session. "Did you enjoy the last assignment?" She asked.

I did! It actually surprised me how much I enjoyed it. At first, I wasn't sure but as soon as was alone I couldn't help getting started. It did take some time finding the best light and position though.

"The photos are very good and I can clearly see your colouring and personality shining through. Did you have a chance to reflect on your own face and body?"

I told her that I had, and then she continued. "What surprised you the most?"

What surprised me? I don't look too bad for my age. My hair looks healthy though my skin is a little bit sallow and I don't like my teeth, they look a bit yellow. However, I like my eyes.

"If I could show you how to bring out even more sparkle to your eyes and make your teeth look whiter, would that be of interest to you?"

Absolutely.

"I want you to be ready and fully aware that it's possible to bring out a healthier complexion and radiance by the choice of colour next to your face. However, I think your skin routine needs improving. What products are you currently using?"

Soap and water to wash my face, and a shampoo bar for my hair.

"Have you checked the ingredients?"

I have, they are natural and animal friendly too.

"The reason I'm asking is because your skin seems very dry around your forehead as well as your nose area, and sometimes this is due to the ingredients in the products we use. You see, just because it says natural doesn't mean the ingredients are good or safe for you or the environment. After all, lead is natural and so is crude oil, but neither are beneficial to apply to your body."

But surely, they wouldn't put dangerous ingredients like those in beauty products, would they?

"Unfortunately, some companies do."

What ingredients shall I avoid?

"There is a long list, which I can send to you. But for the time being try avoiding petroleum-based ingredients such as mineral oil; or anything that contain SLS's and SLES's which lathers excessively; as well as highly scented products. Looking at the area where your skin looks most dry it's likely to be your shampoo."

So, these products would not just have been touching my skin, but also disposed in the water system!

"Yes. It's sad isn't it? What we think is good and safe, is not necessarily great for us or the environment. All I can say is that you need to check the ingredients. I'll forward the list."

Thank you, very thoughtful. But what about products? What do you recommend?

Bridget said she recommended a couple of products and would send some samples for me to try.

Amazing, thank you!

"Let's analyse your photos now. Can you see? I have posted some images in our group. Sharing my screen with you now."

I just need to refresh the page. I clicked F5 and there they were. Seven images - Three of my face with various colours around it; three body images with added patterns on top and an image depicting lines, scribbles and colours in various thickness'.

What does this mean?

"I have created a few colour charts that will help you weed your wardrobe as well as focus your shopping in the future. Let me explain."

Okay.

"First, take a look the three portraits and tell me which one makes your eyes sparkle the most."

The first image, I think. Or perhaps the third… I like the third colour palette the most.'

"What about the second image?"

No, I don't enjoy those colours at all. They are a little bit… wishy washy.

"Look again and this time tell me, where does your teeth look the whitest?"

All of a sudden, I could see what Bridget was trying to show me. The first colour chart made my teeth look less yellow.

Wow! By the look of things my favourite colour spectrum doesn't suit me or my complexion. Why is this?

"Well, your skin tone and hair colour are cool not warm. When you wear camel, orange and any other warm hue, these colours will reflect on your skin tone, rather than compliment you. Therefore, the colour, or garment for that matter, will arrive before you. Even worse, warm colours will make you look less alive."

Wow! I exclaimed. *A great way to get sympathy then ... wearing the wrong colour. Now I know why people keep asking me if I'm okay when I wear my Orange anorak. I've been looking half dead.*

"It's good that you can see this. The whole purpose when it comes to colour analysis is to know how to bring out a healthy-looking self. By the way, and you might have noticed, pink lips will make your teeth appear whiter."

Aha, a natural solution for incorporating my pink brand colour in what I wear. How about the second image? I don't like those colours, but now I can see that they are better than orange, beige and yellow.

"These are your neutral colours. Colours that represent you naturally in depth as well as brightness. Retailers carry staple items in these hues from one season to another, which makes it easier to create and maintain your capsule wardrobe."

Capsule Wardrobe...I can't wait!

"The real opportunity for success lies within the person and not in the job."

Zig Ziglar

To Be Inspired

As we continued our session scrutinising the various colour combinations, I realised that I had been shopping for outfits that were popular rather than what actually suited me personally.

I shook my head whilst mumbling. *What a waste of money.*

"Rose, don't be hard on yourself. You are doing great. Remember this is why you are doing this - to grow in confidence and to create good habits. Now, are you ready to dig deeper to find what suits you?"

I nodded, and she continued.

"Take a look at the other images…Let's start with the lines and squiggles. Do you know what these represent?"

I paused for a second and replied. *Anything to do with patterns?*

"Correct. By studying your face, I have established the best patterns that suits you naturally. Look at the relationship between your eyes and your mouth. They are following the same direction."

I looked closely and could see that the corner of my outer eyes was not horizontally in line with my inner. And when I smiled, my cheeks pulled the corner of my mouth up towards my temples.

My smile is like a banana! I exclaimed.

"More like a Cheshire Cat. You have a happy face that's reflecting a strong signature pattern."

Bridget asked if I ever found it difficult buying shift dresses or fitted jackets. I confided that this was the case and that I preferred separate tops and bottoms to dresses. *Though, when I find a dress that fits, I wear it to death.*

"Have you ever wondered why this is?"

You mean why I wear a dress until it falls apart? I asked

"It's connected, but more to do with why you find it difficult to wear a dress in the first place. Do you know?"

I'm a funny shape?

"Not funnier than the rest of us." Smiling, she continued. "Your back neck to waist is shorter than 'regular' and as you have long legs in comparison, fitted dresses and other items, like fitted tops probably fight to stay in place. Have you ever noticed that some armholes seem to be too large on you?"

Not sure, but I remember that when I wear a summer dress that has straps, I am forever trying to hoist the straps back up, as these always fall off my shoulders.

"Any other item that you can think of?"

Yes, buying swimming costumes. When the bust fit well, the straps always fall down or the crotch cuts me in half. I would much rather wear a tankini.

"Here's the thing. Your back neck to waist is shorter than your seat area, and so are your arms compare to your legs. Purchasing a fitted garment in a regular size will always be a challenge. What you are doing, focusing on separates, is absolutely right. Check out the petite range next time you shop for a fitted jacket or top."

Petite. Really?

"Yes, your upper body follow petite measurements."

What other surprise do you have for me?

"You have a great posture."

Really? Thank you... No one ever mentioned that before!'

"You have, and it serves you well."

What else? I liked what I was hearing. My confidence seems to grow with every affirmation.

"By studying your face shape, your posture and checking the position of your bust point, I can tell you what neck line suits you best. And, there is a particular trouser leg that flatters your body balance really well. However, you might not want to draw attention to certain areas, so, before we continue, I need to know what you wish to emphasise, or if there is anything you wish to hide."

Now I was even more curious. *'Emphasise and hide… That's possible?'* I asked.

"By combining clothes, shapes, textures and colours in a certain way you can create an optical illusion that guides the onlooker to areas of interest. You are in charge here. Providing that you know what you want people to look at and that you know what to do." She continued. "When it comes to your personal image, what features do you want people to look at and to remember?"

I like my eyes, my long neck, my waist and my flat tummy. But I don't like my legs. Especially not my knees and ankles. My feet are okay though.

Bridget continued to explain what necklace length would be most flattering on me and what size as well as shape to focus on. She also showed me what hem length to embrace on skirts as well as trousers, but then she stopped and said.

"Can you see and feel what items of clothing are your best friends?"

I have far too much 'stuff' in my wardrobe that doesn't enhance me, so, I definitely know what isn't a best friend.

"I think you're ready to start focusing on finding what your best friends look like."

She continued. "I have recorded this session and will post a link in our group, as well as some guidelines on what we have covered today. These will help you focus on your next assignment – The Wardrobe Weed"

"My Best Friend is the one who brings out the best in me."

Henry Ford

You're My Best Friend

The following two weeks were going to be packed with work commitments as well as self-discovery assignments. Bridget had left a voice message and emailed a check list of how to start the wardrobe weeding process, which looked like a combination of a spa retreat and bootcamp, but with some quirky personal development added on top.

I prewarned her that due to this amazing new contract it was unlikely that I would be able to finish my latest assignment in a week. *I only have the weekends, so, I think it will take me a month.*

"It's your journey, and you set the timeframe. However, as your coach and co-pilot, we need to regroup in two weeks, making sure you are progressing in the right direction and finishing on time. Let's put a date in our diary right away."

We settled on mid-month, which by then, we would have worked together for six weeks.

It was Saturday when I managed to read through the email Bridget sent earlier in the week.

"Dear Rose, now the unleashing 'finding you' will commence in earnest. You have already discarded clothes that's seen better days, and you should be left with items that you either love wearing or haven't worn for a while.

By embracing this assignment, you will find out why this is.

Let's start by checking what you need to prepare.
To ensure you truly understand what suits you best, the following three must be in place:

1. **Your bust point and waist position** – make sure you wear your best fitting lingerie. It might be necessary to invest in new items
2. **A mirror** – you need to see a reflection of how you move
3. **Designated space for clothes that need to be discarded** – one area for clothes that are to be donated; a second area for clothes that are almost right but need altering; and a third area for clothes that are hardly worn but could be sold at a dress agent or on eBay.

When these are in order, you need to create an inspiring environment.

So, when you are ready - this is what I recommend:

- Put on a favourite piece of music
- Light a candle
- Have your favourite drink to hand

- Wear your best fitting lingerie
- Open up the wardrobe that holds your favourite clothes and remove these and place them on your bed, or hang on a separate clothes rail (if you have one)
- Find and put on your favourite outfit, your 'go-to-outfit', the one you would wear should you be invited out for a friendly get-together
- Focusing on what you have learned so far, look in the mirror and ask yourself:

❖ What do I see?
❖ How do I feel wearing it?
❖ Does it highlight my best features?
❖ Is it still my friend?

Next step:
If one item is a friend and the other's not, you need to say goodbye to the bad and embrace the good.

Next!

- Try on something else
- Go through the same procedure as previously, asking yourself if it's worth keeping
- Continue until there are no items left to try on.

You should now be left with half the content than when you started off.

Add these items to the Wardrobe Inventory and take a new picture of what your fresh wardrobe looks like, then, post both images with the hashtag #wardrobes in our group and make sure to tag me. That's how I know you have finished. When I've seen it, I'll send you the next assignment.

Enjoy, be inspired and have focused fun.

Bridget."

I embraced every single delicious point. Trying on trousers, skirts, dresses, tops, blazers, jerseys, blouses, coats, shoes, belts, necklaces… Adding the ones that made me look and feel my best to the inventory. Everything was scrutinised and at the end they were either hanging back in the wardrobe or discarded according to Bridget's instructions.

By the time Toby returned from another of his diving adventures with Andrew, I was busy scrutinising my image in the mirror and checking the fit of a dress that I had hardly worn.

"Hi! You look like a woman on a mission. Are you having fun?"

Oh yes! I exclaimed. *Focused fun for sure! Did you know, I have been wearing the wrong clothes for over a decade? And the reason is to do with fit rather than colour or style.*

I'm a combination of regular and petite, which is why I have struggled wearing dresses and this is probably why I always fidget when I wear the wrong shape.

"No, I didn't know that's why you fidget."

Ha, ha. Well, it's not the only reason, but it has a great impact. I pause, look at him and ask. *How was your day?*

"Good in some ways but disheartening in others. My deep-sea treasure turned out to be plastic rather than gold. I think the previous storm must have dislocated a deposit of rubbish from somewhere."

That's so sad to hear. Well done for taking action.

What's for dinner?"

Haven't got a clue.

"What shall I make for us? "

Surprise me.

"If you want to live a happy life, tie it to a goal, not to people or objects."

Albert Einstein

In the Right Direction

After finishing the assignment, I posted an image of my svelte wardrobe and tagged Bridget, after which she sent me a private voice mail.

"Rose, well done! I'm currently out of the country, on my way to Manila, and will be in touch as soon as I've landed."

It took another day before she responded. "Apologies for the delay – I've just settled in and for the next couple of weeks I'll be asleep when you are awake. Your next assignment will be posted in a moment. Enjoy and be inspired."

In her post she asked me to take pictures of every single item of clothing as well as accessories that I'd written down in the inventory followed by sharing these with her. Which I did - all 67 of them.

At our catch up the following Tuesday, I assured Bridget that I was on track and she asked if I was ready to share my thoughts around my wardrobe with her.

She explained: "I have entered every item you shared with me so far into a picture gallery. Have you received the invite to open the link?"

Got it.

"Let's start with the first item. What can you tell me about this one?"

It's a top that I love to wear when I go out for something to eat. Casual but smart.

"When you wear it how do you feel?"

Comfortable...

"Anything else?"

Relaxed.

"Is this how you like to feel when you go out or would you like to achieve something else?"

Interesting question. I paused and looked at Bridget when I answered.

I wouldn't mind looking more polished, more elegant.

"What does more polished look like to you?"

More put-together, less bland.

"So, what else do you wear with it?"

I scrolled down the photo gallery.

The jeans next to the navy dress, and the purple cardigan are my go-to items.

"Okay. Why do you go for these?"

I told her that they felt comfortable to wear and that they made me feel approachable.

"Do you accessorise?"

Accessorise... No, not really. I find it difficult to know how to do it, without looking like a Christmas tree. I love wearing earrings and I have plenty of beautiful jewellery that Toby has given me and some that I've inherited. But I don't think they are me.

We covered plenty more and I mentioned that there were other items lying around at home. Items that I loved but hadn't worn for many years; more tops that I hadn't been able to add to the list; duplicates which I didn't know what to do with. I plucked up some courage and asked her:

So, when can we start to create my capsule wardrobe?

"Now that you are asking, I think we are ready. But first, you need to create a habit of analysing the clothes in your wardrobe and decide if these are your absolute best friends." Sharing her screen, she explained: Use this type of spider gram as your starting point."

I looked at the spider diagram on the shared screen, and Bridget continued to explain the process.

```
              Trousers
       Coat
                          Skirt

Jacket      Favourite Top      Shorts

       Cardigan
                          Jersey
          Accessories  Footwear
```

"Start off by writing down your favourite top in the circle. You should know it by now. Continue by adding as many items as you would wear with this particular item. Trousers, skirts, leggings, culottes, shoes, boots, necklace, hat, earrings … your choice, your capsule wardrobe. Then take one of the additional items, the trousers perhaps, and repeat this process. This will give you a clear understanding how many options you have per item.

The more possibilities you have the better the friend.
I was busy taking notes, when she paused looking sincerely at me before she continued.

"Do you feel up for this?"

I do. And I promise that I will be ready for our next session in two weeks' time... Bridget, I hope you don't mind me asking, are you working in Manila?

"I don't mind you asking and no, I'm not working. I'm volunteering for a charity that's close to my heart."

Really, in Manila?

"Yes, I sponsor a few very talented teenagers so they can go to college. They live on a dumpsite outside Manila, and they are incredibly talented, but outside the education system due to lack of finances as well as where they live.

They live on a rubbish tip?

"They do, but it doesn't define who they are. They too have hope and a future and I'm doing what I can to give talented young people like these confidence in being who they were meant to be."

You are amazing!

"We are all amazing when we follow our heart. Especially when we do something about something that makes us uncomfortable. And, if you want to understand what systemised recycling looks like, this is the place to visit."

I didn't know what to say other than to ask Bridget for more information. She promised to forward a link.

"I'll forward the capsule wardrobe diagram and instructions later. This will be your next piece of homework. But before you get started, make sure to treat yourself to something nice, you are definitely worth a treat."

I will, and for the first time in many years I'm going to find something new to wear, something that reflects who I am, and I'm looking forward to finding it!

"Be who you are and say what you want, for those who mind don't matter, and those who matter don't mind."

Dr. Seuss

Here I Am

The day started off really well with a successful presentation to the board of directors. They could see the benefits of incorporating a water recycling system in a sustainable work environment.

I thought it was going to take more time for the whole board to agree, but there was no need to worry.

At break I went off to do an errand and as I walked past a recently opened shoe shop, I noticed a nice pair of espadrilles in the window. I decided to go and try them on, and if they fitted me well, I would make them my treat. As I slipped them on, I remembered Bridget's advice.

"When trying new things on ask yourself three questions:
1. Do I love it enough to take it home?
2. Has it got any friends?
3. Can I care for it?

If your answer is a resounding 'Yes' then take it home. If you are uncertain, ask for your right to return. When you are back home, check for 'friends'; don't decide right away but sleep on it, and if you wonder why you purchased it the following morning – return it!"

I did love the shoes enough to take them home. Made with more than 95% natural materials, I felt true to my eco-values. Buying new shoes and not second hand, has always been important to me. Something that my granddad had instilled in me. Also, I knew they would work with most of my spring/ summer wardrobe - I couldn't wait to wear them.

Leaving the shop, I happened to bump in to a friend whose book club I used to be part of - a group of women with whom I had never felt comfortable being around. Perhaps it was just a feeling, but it soon transpired that my gut instinct had been correct.

Hi Marie, how are you?

"Hi Rose…You look different. I hardly recognised you."

Really? Thank you. I think.

She looked me up and down, and I had a feeling that she wasn't pleased.

"Yes, but I don't know what it is."

I'm finding me. I said. *I've found my confident image and I'm having a great time.*

"Hmm. I don't like it." She said "I'm not sure if it suits you."

As always, I couldn't believe what I had heard, as Marie had this hurtful way about her. This time, instead of being silent I actually surprised myself.

Well, to be honest, I'm not doing this to please you. I'm doing this for me. And your comment, trying to stop me from feeling great about myself, is hurtful. Marie, my wish for you is that you find happiness too. Without looking back, although I was curious to see her face, I left.

My word! Where did that courage come from?

My heart was pounding and it felt good to be able to walk away tall, and with confidence.

I could hear Bridget saying, *'That's not a good friend'* and I giggled to myself when I reaffirmed the fact that not everyone and everything is a good friend.

I returned to my office and finished off the document that I was working on. At five o'clock I switched the system off, packed my belongings to go home and prepared for another 'me' weekend. Without feeling guilty whilst Toby and Andrew were away at a Christian conference, I knew exactly how to spend it. Saturday daytime I would be busy creating my capsule wardrobe. Saturday evening, I was going out with the girls and Sunday lunch, after Church, I was catching up with Elena. It was going to be focused fun for sure.

Oh no! I really think Bridget is living in my head.

At 6am my alarm went off. As I had a full day planned, I only allocated 30 minutes for my Miracle Morning (something else Elena had introduced me to) followed by a brisk walk and a shower before enjoying my breakfast on the balcony. Now, I was more than ready to embrace the task of creating a capsule wardrobe.

Bridget had asked me to focus on spring and summer items and put the out-of-season clothes and accessories in the 'hibernation unit', which I did. But as I glanced at the items in my wardrobe, I could see that there were far too many clothes that looked the same. Five ecru T-shirts;

three fleece tops; six pairs of jeans; three purple cardigans – some more bobbly than others.

I read her instruction. "Now that you are left with items that suit you best, we are going to encourage two things.

- To create a 'Boutique Wardrobe' – your capsule
- To create a shopping list – pinpointing any gaps

Your capsule will not be static. Items will wear out and when they do you can easily replace these with something fresh to go with what's remaining in your closet.

All you have to do is go back over what you've learned about the why's and how's."

The whole purpose of creating a capsule wardrobe became clear as soon as I started filling in the blank spaces. Suddenly it felt as if a yoke had been lifted from my shoulders.

I re-read Bridget's instructions. "Where it says 'neutral' – these are your safe colours; 'accents' are your complimentary hues - your fashion colours if you like; and where it says 'personal' it means just that – something that brings Rose out."

Printing out two copies of the 'Capsule Wardrobe Companion' I started off by adding items that worked well together. I thoroughly enjoyed seeing my wardrobe with fresh eyes. Contrary to my beliefs, I did have some nice items to work with and some gaps to be filled too.

This is good. I like what I see.

As I forwarded a copy of the 'companion' to Bridget, just as she had asked, I started to plan what to wear that evening.

I'm going to wear the linen trousers that I forgot I had and the cashmere top that Toby gave me last Christmas.

I'd never worn the top before because I didn't like the way it looked on me. However, now I knew that was due to the neckline. To make it work for me, I added a dangly necklace, just as Bridget had taught me. Once again, I could hear her voice in my head.

"V-necks are your best friend. If the neckline on a top doesn't work, you can try creating an optical illusion by adding a necklace."

The espadrilles, my 'treat', looked great on my feet and made me feel assured yet comfortable. I applied some blusher and lip gloss (pink tinted) and checked my new hairstyle; another treat that Bridget had helped me decide upon. I felt on top of the world!

Here I am. I said to myself as I walked into town to meet up with the girls.

BONUS: download, for free, the Capsule Wardrobe Companion using this link:
https://2b-inspired.com/capsulewardrobecompanion/

"Everything that irritates us about others can lead us to an understanding of ourselves."

C.G. Jung

Awareness Unleashed

My journey of self-discovery was coming to an end. With only a month to go, I felt as if I was ready to take on the world. My wardrobe and the way I felt about myself started to become an extension of my innermost values and beliefs.

I told Bridget this when I saw her the following Tuesday.

"You make me so happy hearing this. Thank you!"

I mean it. It has changed my life. Surely, there can't be much more for us to do?

"We are almost there. Remember, I've promised to leave you with a mobile app containing your whole capsule wardrobe. To help you stay focused on what to purchase so that you don't buy duplicates of what you already have. Also, there are a couple of items that we need to discuss. And then there is a shopping list with recommendations for you to purchase as well as a few outfits for me to create for you."

As if it was possible, my face lit up even more. *Wow*!

"All in all, you have claimed a good part of your confident signature style. But today, let's do a Q&A session. I'm pretty sure you have encountered something that you wish to ask me…Yes?"

I thought for a short second and proceeded with a thought that's been burning on my mind for some time. *Why did my favourite top go bobbly so quickly?*

"That's a great question. One which I get asked many times. I first need to know what fibres are used to make the top. Do you know where to look?"

The washing instructions, I think…

"So, what does it say?"

50% Cashmere and 50% wool.

"Does it say lamb's wool? Or new wool or perhaps merino?"

No, just wool.

"Okay, then that's most likely to be 'recycled wool'. Which will explain the bobbling even more."

What do you mean? I thought 'recycled wool' would be better.

"For environmental reasons, recycling is great, but certain fabrics, especially recycled wool, have been shredded and feels harder as the fibres would have gone through either a dry-cleaning process, which uses harsh chemicals, or washed with a lanolin stripping detergent."

I see… So, if my top had been created using new wool or Merino, it would have lasted longer?

"Basically, yes, however it's not guaranteed. The cashmere could be of an inferior quality. A short fibre is less resilient, which is typical for recycled materials, and these would bobble more than longer fibres...Where did you buy this top?"

In the sale, it was a great bargain. Reduced from £90 to £39.

"How many times have you worn it?"

No more than 5 times. It went bobbly straight away.

Bridget was taking down some notes, when I continued with another question.

So, would 100% polyester be a better solution?

"That depends on the garment. What item do you have in mind?"

My fleece tops.

"Do you wear them for work?"

I have worn one for work, but it's not a very flattering shape. Now I only wear it when hiking or gardening.

"I see, is it okay with you if we recap on how far you have defined your signature style?"

Absolutely.

"Your values are based on harmony, compassion and clarity, and your business expertise provides corporations with sustainable business practices that will take the stress away from environmental mishaps."

That's my aim – to make more people aware of what the global impact will be if we don't change our habits. And I do want to wear my passion.

"Fair enough. So, what made you buy the fleece top?"

What made me buy it? All of my eco-conscious colleagues seem to wear fleeces, it's lightweight; it's easy to wash and it's made of recycled plastic bags so it's a great eco-friendly item. Or am I wrong?

"Not wrong, but depending on what's most important for you. Is it recycling or being eco-friendly?"

I like to incorporate both.

Okay, let me explain about fibres in more detail:

- Plant or animal-derived fibres are biodegradable but synthetics are not
- When you wash plant-based fibres in water they expand and become stronger
- Animal-derived fibres, such as cashmere, wool and silk, don't benefit from being washed in warm soapy water
- Cotton and Bamboo are not as eco-friendly as we believe – unless grown organically and without using pesticides
- Bleached fabrics harm the environment more than unbleached

- Most bright and colourful items have been bleached before using synthetic dyes
- Polyester, Acrylic, Polyamide, Nylon and similar synthetics are basically plastic
- All the fluff you see left in the tumble dryer are fibres from your clothes – which means they are wearing out quicker with each tumble.

So much to consider!

"They're just a few facts, which might help you rethink what you wear and what to invest in?"

Didn't you mention previously that some beauty products contain plastic?

"I did. Rose, if you want to make a conscious difference and be congruent with your values and what you purchase, like: clothes, beauty products, stationary, buildings, cars as well as food. You need to understand what it is that you are buying."

Thank you, so, back to my fleece, why does it smell so badly after I washed it?

"To be honest I don't know why yours does. It could be the detergent; or the washing machine not draining old stagnant water properly. Though, it's most likely because it's made out of synthetics and these attracts odours quicker than organic fibres."

I'm definitely put off wearing it now. How about my cashmere top?

"What about it?"

I love it but I know it's an expensive item which makes me feel guilty wearing it.

"I can understand that. But compared it with the fleece. Is it a friend or foe?"

It's a friend for sure.

"So, how many times have you worn this cashmere jumper and do you know how much it cost?"

I thought about it and I soon realised that I have worn it more than 10 times. It was a gift from Toby, so I didn't know the cost. I told Bridget this.

"And the fleece?"

Maybe 30 times…

"I want you to think about the meaning of a true bargain. We'll analyse what it means in our next session."

Brilliant, I look forward to it.

"Rose."

Yes

"Wear what makes you happy. Don't feel guilty wearing something that's nice or expensive. You want to embrace what compliments you, rather than lock it away… Don't you?"

Yes, I do!

"Inside every human being there are treasures to unlock."

Mike Huckabee

A True Bargain

Over the weekend we entertained family and friends nonstop. It was Andrews 18th birthday and everyone who came said what a wonderful celebration it was. For once I had found it easy getting dressed as my wardrobe had become more inspiring – my own boutique.

I chose to wear my go-to favourite outfit - linen trousers, cashmere top and my new espadrilles. I even added a chunkier necklace. *I am getting brave.* My confidence had grown so much and when I received a compliment, which happened a lot, I was able to say 'Thank you' rather than just brush it away. As much as I love this outfit, I feel restricted. Plus, I don't want to be remembered for always wearing the same. As nice as it is, it will wear out one day. *Bring on Bridget!*

When Bridget and I met the following Tuesday she asked about my weekend and if I had thought about our previous session?

I mentioned the lovely compliments I had received and that I felt as if I've found my confidence as well as signature style, but that I needed more outfits.

"I've put some outfits together for you, which I believe will inspire you and embrace the possibilities finding different options to wear. Let me upload an example now."

I refreshed my screen and there it was, my very first outfit created by Bridget.

Wow! You put those together. I never thought of doing that!

"Can you see why?"

Yes, I can! I felt very proud of myself for seeing it. *The shape of the blouse will enhance my figure as well as my face shape; the colour will make my eyes pop; the skirt will end at the most flattering part of my leg; and the shoes are my current favourite. But I would never have put the top and skirt together. The skirt is casual and the top is pretty... interesting... And the leather jacket is very old. I have had it since before Andrew was born.*

"Your leather jacket is perfect. It looks as if it's truly loved. Not shabby, just loved and cared for. There is absolutely nothing wrong wearing a pretty item with something casual, providing it enhances a healthy confident 'you'. The onlooker will be drawn to your face, probably check to make sure that what you wear on your feet compliments your whole look. The leather jacket will be a pleasant surprise for the right client, your ideal client. Wearing this outfit will reflect confidence as well strength and you will clearly be remembered in a positive way."

Exciting!

"It is, isn't it." She paused and continued. "Now, what about those tops. Have you been able to ponder which one's a true bargain?"

I have...

"How about your 'sales bargain'?"

It's probably not such a bargain after all.

"And the one you have been wearing lately?"

It might be, though I don't know how much it cost. You tell me, I don't mind finding out.

"Take a look at this diagram:

Top	Cost	Times Worn	Cost per wear £ divided by T.W.	Bargain?
Polyester Fleece Top	£45	20	£45/20 = £2.25p	
'Sale' Cashmere Top	£39	5	£39/5 = £7.80	
100% Cashmere Top	£120	10	£120/10 = £12	
Linen Trousers	£30	20	£30/20 = £1.50	
Leather Jacket	£200	200 +	£200/200 = 1p	
Wedge Espadrilles	£80	15	£80/15 = £5.33	
Cotton Blouse	£29	5	£29/5 = £5.80	

What are your thoughts? Which one is a true bargain?"

Though I don't want to keep it, it's my fleece top. Only £2.25 pence per wear!

"And the other two?"

We discussed each item and finished off by adding the clothes from the 'Outfit Creator' to the chart, and it soon transpired that a sale item isn't necessarily a true bargain, especially if it was hardly worn.

Bridget then asked if I thought my most expensive top had more life in it?

Yes, it hardly shows any wear or tear and I absolutely love wearing it. It's likely that I'll wear it until it falls apart. That would make it a truly great bargain, wouldn't it?

"I believe so, providing you care for it correctly.

What do you recommend?

"If you want it to last as long as possible, you shouldn't wash it, but if you must, only use lukewarm water and a detergent formulated solely for cashmere."

Not wash it!

"It's best if you could just hang it out to air as often as possible and only surface clean it to remove any spillage."

Oh. I never heard of that before.

Remember what we discussed in our last session? Plant based fibres such as Cotton, Linen and Viscos benefit from being washed in very hot water, but animal fibres like Cashmere, Wool and Silk, are protein rich, and these don't like water in the same way. Moths are another reason for airing your clothes.

Well I never... Not only will I care for my favourite top, but I will also care for the environment by not washing it as often as I've been used to. But what about armpits?

"Just make sure to air your clothes as often as you can, and wear a light weight, washable, top next to your skin."

Okay, I'll bear that in mind. Thank you, Bridget.

"Rose, it's my total pleasure sharing my knowledge with you."

She continued. "From now on I'll be doing most of the work. Adding items to your shopping list as well as creating your perfect capsule and compiling outfits to compliment your signature style. But before we say goodbye for today, I want you to give me two items from your current wardrobe that I can work around. What two do you want to wear more often?"

My navy wool crepe dress and... the Periwinkle linen T-shirt.

"Fab! Let's see what I can come up with. Meanwhile, and if you have any questions, just message me."

Okay, I will.

"Confidence happens with experience, there is no shortcut."

Berith Sandgren-Clarke

Not 'The End'

So much had changed in these past ten weeks. Positively changed! I had finally understood why certain items of clothing didn't do me any justice, and what a 'best friend' should look and feel like.

Most of the black sacks that were filling our spare bedroom had been disposed of and in the right direction.

- Good quality items, that didn't do me any justice but where 'reasonably' trendy or classic, had gone to a dress agent
- Items that the dress agent wouldn't take for various reasons, have been donated to my local charity shop
- Those that looked too tired for the charity shop had been recycled, as I was told that they would sell these by the weight, to a company who in return would recycle the cloth
- Items that I thought had been wrong, though Bridget had reassured me were good, had been incorporated into my boutique wardrobe
- Only a few items were left for me to ponder if they were worth keeping. My corset being one.

Looking at what was left, my wardrobe was a delight, and getting dressed each morning was inspiring. My style wasn't much different from work and play. Some of my pre loved work clothes, that were a little bit sad, I now wore for gardening or other leisurely activities. I had learned what to look for when I shopped as well as how to update an old friend. And, I knew how and what to pack when travelling with work as well as leisure. My professional and personal image was true to me - my signature style.

When I logged in to our penultimate session, I felt a combined sensation of sadness and excitement.

"Rose! Can you believe it, 90 days are almost over and we are nearing the end? Only a couple of assignments for you to do and then you should be free to take on the world without me. How do you feel?"

I feel elated yet sad. I have truly enjoyed my self-discovery journey. The fear I had in the beginning, a feeling that I would be confused and lost, hasn't emerged at all. I know who I am! I'm loving me and I know how to maintain my style. It has, just as you said, become a habit. But I will miss our sessions. I know I will.

"Same here. I will miss you too but it's not the end. We will meet up for our final in two weeks and then a follow up in a couple of months. And, you do know about the 'Outfit Creator Service', don't you?

I do, but surely there will be an additional charge?

"Yes, there is an additional charge, however, you probably won't need me in the foreseeable future. But I'm here should you want my advice. Just in case, and for your own benefit, I want you to continue to update your 'Boutique' on the app, with items that you purchase, add pictures to it, as well as take away anything you no longer wear. This will allow you to focus on what to invest in. Avoiding duplicates and 'bad friends.' Also, I will be able to check to see what's in there should you be in contact. We are connected until you request otherwise."

Bridget continued. "I have a secret online group where my clients share their purchases and ask for advice from each other. Every week I share a golden nugget, sometimes two, and once a month I hold a seminar that focus on a specific topic. It's a subscription platform which you are entitled to join for free for one month. Would this be of benefit to you now or do you want to wait for a month or two?"

I like to dive right in. I replied without hesitating, it just felt so natural to continue.

"Excellent, I'll invite you as soon as we have finished today's session."

Okay... You mentioned that there are a couple of extra assignments for me to do. What are they?

"Do you know a good photographer?"

I do.

"I want you to make an appointment with them this week if you can, because you need to have a handful of professional pictures taken. Signature images of you that will represent you in a media environment - especially LinkedIn. If you have a website, which I know you do, now is the time to update it with your brand colours as well as fresh photos."

When do I need this done by?

"Updating your website may take more than two weeks but if you could focus on having your profile picture taken and uploaded on LinkedIn then that would make a huge difference to your credentials and confidence."

I'll get on it as soon as possible. Anything else?

"Make sure you do some market research. Check out your competitors. Study what they do and discern what makes you different from them. Then, let your signature style shine. And remember, there are plenty of experts out there to help you. If you want my recommendation, I have contacts. Just ask."

The following week was a blur. I attended a big sustainability exhibition in London which meant that I stayed over a couple of nights at one of the big hotels. As tired as I felt I did manage to do the 'Confidence Calculator' again, which Bridget wanted to discuss at our final session.

The truth was there to be seen, black on white and clearly defined. I had found me. My personal style is now congruent with my values, vision and mission. I've created a signature style that could easily be maintained.

-

When we met, I said: *I can see and feel it! My confidence in who I am, who my ideal client is and what my business stands for is aligned and based on a solid foundation.*

"Comparing the two assessments, what's obvious to you?"

I have come a long way. Look at the difference!!! The three pillars support my vision; I'm confident in who I am, I actually love getting dressed; I know and understand my values as well as my ideal client's; and I have a business brand that represents me... or the other way around.

"Does it matter which way around?"

No, it only matters that I'm finally accepting that it's okay to be recognized and memorable - for having a signature style. No need to pretend to be someone else.

"Does it feel good?"

I could feel happy tears welling up as I answered her question. *It feels amazing! I'm confidently free to be me.*

I continued. *Bridget, have you seen my new profile picture on LinkedIn?*

"No, I haven't' Let me open up a new tab... Look at you!!! When did you upload this and didn't tell me?"

This morning. I did send you an email but I must admit it wasn't until 3pm.

"You look confident and approachable. I think this was your goal? So, I'll take it as confirmation that I have delivered what you were hoping for."

Oh yes, you certainly have.

"Rose, every year I attend a global conference for women who wish to empower each other as well as contribute in society. It's called 'Destined for Bigger Things'. Next year it will be held in Barcelona and I would love to see you there?"

I will see you in person?

"I'm the keynote speaker so you will see me for sure, but I want to meet you in person. Elena normally attend these events, so the two of you could perhaps travel together maybe even share a room. Can you make it?"

I'll put it in my diary for sure.

"Fantastic! By the way, let me know if you ever visit The Cotswolds, I love to buy you a coffee."

How are you fixed for next week?

> *"YOU are your own brand, and how you manage your personal brand can make or break your career."*
>
> *Aliza Licht*

What Next?

There are a number of hints and tips covered in this book and it's likely that you have questions or thoughts about the process mentioned.

I recommend that you check out 2B-inspired website for the latest updates which hopefully will give you a feel for what I can offer you. **https://2B-inspired.com**

The goal in writing this book was to inspire you to explore and take action finding you. If you have any questions about *Define Your Signature Style* you can email me personally at **Berith@2B-inspired.com**

*** OFFER ***

Also, if you feel this book would help someone else, I would like to invite you to leave a review on Amazon, spreading the word that it's ok to invest in your personal image especially if you wish to become more

If you leave a review of *Define Your Signature Style* and send me a screen shot or a link to the review, I would like to offer you a **FREE** 60-minute Signature Style Audit (normally it's 20 minutes).

Seeing and hearing that you are ready to claim your signature style inspires me to do what I do.

Most of all, thank you for taking your time reading *Define Your Signature Style – Be Recognised for Who You Are.*

From the bottom of my heart, Thank You!

... in the eye of the beholder

What is classified as beautiful and what's ugly? And, who's the beholder?

Here's my thinking.

Don't get me wrong, there have been ugly things happening in my life, but I have been brought up experiencing beauty in everyday events, through images as well as words of affirmation.

From an early age I learned to appreciate that beauty is all around me, no matter what everyone else was thinking or saying.

My dad, with a cheeky grin on his face, used to introduce himself (and still does occasionally), as "vackra Jan" (Swedish for handsome Jan). And, when someone was commenting on what he was wearing, good or bad, he used to reply with the words "Everything looks great on someone who's already beautiful". He always replied with a positive.

I was raised in a household where beauty and brains were seen as equal. My parents used to tell me I had both, and 55 years later they still do. It's good to be encouraged no matter what age.

Growing up with my parents love and affirmation was fantastic, but it didn't stop me from thinking I wasn't beautiful or clever. Being picked on at school for having red hair and my head in the clouds, I used to feel ugly and stupid, comparing myself with others, thinking they were picked on less and therefore must be more beautiful and cleverer than me.

To get around 'feeling less worthy' I used to copy what they said as well as what they wore. It wasn't until I started to love me for who 'I am' that I gave up trying to copy their behaviour. Don't get me wrong, I can still feel ugly and stupid, but I've learnt to overcome those thoughts with positives and feel blessed for what I have.

Beauty is deep, and sometimes we will hold on to our own for dear life not letting others see it. Just in case we get hurt...

Perhaps you can relate? Perhaps you haven't been brought up being told how to look for beauty around you, or perhaps you feel ashamed wishing that you could hear it said to you more often.

*It's time you realise that **you are the beholder** and believe that beauty is shining brightly from your eyes, skin, mouth and whole being.*

There are several studies to prove that we are drawn to certain 'beauty standards' and that's part of being human. However, for me, knowing that true beauty comes from how we feel about ourselves has given me a passion looking for beauty in everyday life. And you know what, it's everywhere.

Hear this, and believe it - You are beautiful!

If this belief in you is as small as a mustard seed, then that's big enough. You just have to cultivate it by affirmations and self-care. If you believe in the one who *created you, you must pray for an enlightenment to see you as He sees you - **fearfully and wonderfully made.***

Perhaps this is why I do what I do - Encourage women like you to feel beautiful in who they are and inspire them to dress accordingly to their vision and values.

To take charge of being the beholder, and be true to who you are meant to be.

(From 2B-inspired blog post, dated 8th January 2019)

Gratitude

Before I forget, there are a few names I must mention here and now.

Thank you to:

Glenn, for your support and love.

Robin, for inspiring me to write this book.

Kezia, for your wisdom and vision.

Wendy, for your honesty and expertise.

Linda, for your friendship and encouragement.

Gill, for being a most dedicated Savvy Shopper.

Debbie, for being the best business buddy.

Mamma and Pappa, for always believing in me.

My children, for accepting that I'm not perfect.

You, for having read the full story.

Resources

The following links will help you acquire assessments, publications and/ or authors who made it possible for me to write *Define who you are - Be recognised for having a signature style*.

Joel Osteen: https://www.joelosteen.com/

Ryder Carroll: http://www.rydercarroll.com/

Helen Harrison: https://coachingcards.co.uk/contact-us/

Hal Elrod: https://halelrod.com/

Robin Waite: https://www.robinwaite.com/

Women of Contribution:
http://www.womenofcontribution.com/

KCM, Manila:
https://www.facebook.com/KalayaanMinistries/

Confidence Calculator:
https://www.2b-inspired.com/the-assessment

Style Quest:
https://www.2b-inspired.com/style-quest

Wardrobe Inventory:
https://2b-inspired.com/wardrobeinventory/

Capsule Wardrobe Companion:
https://2b-inspired.com/capsulewardrobecompanion/

Praise

About ten years ago, Berith provided me with a color session and wardrobe weeding. It was an eye-opener! I learned so much and she truly saved a lot of time and money on my future clothes shopping excursions because I understood the best styles and colors for me.

My training from Berith helped me to understand what I already had in my wardrobe and, armed with a list of items needed, I could confidently assess the clothes in a store and quickly spot the things that suited me vs spending hours trying things on, wondering if something MIGHT suit me, or just buying the same things I already had.

Recently, I had the pleasure of a Savvy Shopping session with Berith. Just when I thought I knew it all, through Berith's coaching we talked about how our bodies, coloring and style can change over the years. For some of us, perhaps we have started a new career or have retired. A Savvy Shopping session was just the thing that helped me refresh my understanding of who I am, at this time in my life, and to better understand the styles, shapes and colors of clothing that suit me. Berith gave me a fresh new confident attitude after our session. I cannot recommend her enough, her sessions are fun and informative, while providing practical tools to help you make the best fashion decisions. It's time and money very well spent!

Linda Thomson

Berith helped me to sort through my clothes, to remove the tired items and also evaluate if I really needed 3 white linen blouses in different styles!

I removed a lot of items that simply weren't me. Items I had never or hardly ever worn. She taught me to look for 'friends' for a single item, questioning if it did have any other items to wear with it. She also taught me how to find the gaps in my wardrobe, so if I wanted to go clothes shopping, I would have a direction in how to fill the gaps.

I totally trust Berith, she knows my style and knows how to be honest with me when I need it. She is so experienced in so many avenues and highly professional.

'B' has enabled me to be a more confident shopper and dresser and has inspired me to make more of an effort in the way I dress and portray myself to the world.

Mel Reed

I met Berith through a chance encounter: I'd accidentally become a freelancer after being made redundant and was trying my hand at networking. After 35 years' employment, my new status was giving cause for reflection in more ways than one!

I liked Berith's friendly, approachable manner and we bonded instantly. I felt comfortable sharing thoughts and feelings and before long, I asked her to help me update my wardrobe to better suit my new lifestyle. And there my journey began… Almost ten years later, my personal style has evolved and my confidence grown. I regularly use the techniques taught to me by Berith: I weed my own wardrobe and we still have the best fun Savvy Shopping.

Most importantly, she's helped me get to know myself better. As a result, I feel more comfortable and happier with my appearance and this is reflected in comments from friends and partner.

Gill Few

Working with Berith has revolutionised my wardrobe and my thinking! Getting to understand that the capsule wardrobe for my Business Brand didn't mean having to part with old favourites which means I can actually wear the clothes I love to the beach, garden or even to my allotment.

Learning how to combine styles and patterns was illuminating – not least of all what size of pattern and neckline would flatter. Berith chose items I wouldn't have thought about putting together to great effect and feedback.

So now I have: -

- A travelling photo album of my existing clothes and accessories in my boutique wardrobe to refer to when I shop
- A spring-cleaned wardrobe
- Clear understanding of what's lacking in my wardrobe and what's tired and will soon need replacing
- The confidence to walk out of shops if they don't have exactly what I want
- A mantra to use when buying

Choosing outfits has become inspiring not something I struggle with.

Debbie Stewart

About the Author

Firstly, and to let you know, I don't enjoy talking about myself but I can tell you that I have always been curious finding out what makes a woman truly beautiful and I can clearly remember, from a very early age, observing what women were wearing and how they moved.

As my interest in beautification techniques increased, I was creating fashion items for my dolls, practising makeup techniques on their faces as well as my own. I remember very clearly the day, age eight, being sent home from school for wearing too much makeup.

This incident didn't stop me at all. Trying my hands at every subject I considered important to the beatification process, I was soon experimenting cutting my friends' hair, applying makeup and making their clothes.

Visualising becoming a world-famous fashion designer, whilst studying hard and gaining a distinction in flat pattern cutting and textile technology, I was applying for roles in various fashion-related organisations.

Soon I found myself working with a renowned global company, training new staff on how to gain trust whilst recommending and selling beauty products over the counter.

I was excellent at this, but I didn't love it. However, I had a fantastic mentor who taught me the importance of having strong values. The good income gave me the opportunity to play fast and hard. Needless to say, I soon burnt out and found myself in a deep dark place including hospitalisation.

Realising that I desperately needed to recharge whilst pondering on my 'why', the company offered me a sabbatical and gave me as much time as I needed. This is the gift that changed my life.

On a cold and damp November morning I left for England to try something totally different - I became a Swedish au pair. Very clichéd, I know. Improving my English and learning to survive on very little money I quickly fell in love with my adopted country.

Nine months later, I returned to Sweden for a short few months, and as I had met my husband-to-be earlier in the year, I returned the following Autumn to study fashion design in London.

Specialising in pattern cutting and female tailoring, whilst creating five different collections, I graduated with the highest GPA of all graduating students. I did my internship with The Emmanuels (designers of Princess Diana's wedding dress) which I'm sure gave me the confidence to apply for a job as a pattern cutter, working alongside the design department, at what was then the Wallis Fashion Group.

When my daughter was three years old, our family moved away from London. There wasn't much need for my expertise, but after the arrival of my son I decided to use my dormant skills to start my own design company which after a couple of years transformed organically into an image consultancy business.

Using what I knew relating to clothes, beauty and confidence, I realised that I had found my calling - to empower and inspire women to dress confidently according to their values and vision, and to be recognised for having a signature style.

In recent years, and due to global awareness, I have found myself reverting to what my 'Mormor' (maternal grandmother) taught me about quality and sustainability. She was one of a handful of people in Sweden who understood how to mend Persian hand knotted rugs. She had an excellent eye for colour and quality as well as an understanding of how to care for fabrics. To say that she inspired me is an understatement.

So here I am, working globally and online, giving women in business confidence knowing what to wear.

Visit my website:
https://2B-inspired.com/

Contact me via email:
berith@2b-inspired.com

Follow me on LinkedIn:
https://www.linkedin.com/in/berithsc/

Follow me on Instagram:
https://www.instagram.com/2binspired_official/

Further Inspiration

The Power of I am	by Joel Osteen
The Bullet Journal Method	by Ryder Carroll
Value Cards	by Helen Harrison
Miracle Morning	by Hal Elrod
The Secret	by Rhonda Byrne
On Fire	by John O'Leary
The Success Principles	by Jack Canfield
The Triumph of Individual Style	by Carla Mathis
Online Business Startup	by Robin Waite
Go for No	by Fenton/ Waltz
Work Like A Woman	by Mary Portas
The Seasons of Life	by Jim Rohn
Retire Inspire	by Andrew Priestley
The Rules of Life	by Richard Templar
Notes to My Younger Self	by Kezia Luckett
The Bible	

"She is clothed with strength and dignity, and she laughs without fear of the future."

Proverbs 31:25 (NLT)

[Discarding] – with somebody to help?
or just my judgment?

p.53 I can't answer?

The notion of a "client"? + a business

Special stipple shoes + bags.